YES I CAN!

Abdi's Story

ABDI ADEN

ILLUSTRATED BY PAWEL NOWACKI

First published in Australia 2018
by Abdi Aden
Copyright © Abdi Aden 2018

ISBN: 978-0-6481581-0-3

All rights reserved. No part of this book may be reproduced or transmitted in any form or by any means, electronic or mechanical, including photocopying, recording or by any information storage and retrieval system, without prior permission in writing from the publisher. The Australian Copyright Act 1968 (The Act) allows a maximum of one chapter or 10 per cent of any book, whichever is the greater, to be photocopied by any educational institution for its educational purposes provided that the educational institution (or the body that administers it) has given a remuneration notice to Copyright Agency Limited (CAL) under the Act.

www.facebook.com/inspired.abdi

ACKNOWLEDGEMENT

I would like to thank and in no particular order Sherryl, Luke, and Suzanne. Your creative flare, knowledge and support in helping get this together is absolutely amazing. Pawel, thank you your drawings bought the story to life.

ABOUT THE AUTHOR

Abdi Aden is a storyteller and author from *Shining – The Story of a Lucky Man*, who is also known for his advocacy for human rights. Since 2001 he has loved working with young people both as a Youth Worker and now as a Public Speaker at Primary and Secondary Schools across the country.

A highlight was in 2007 when Abdi received the Victorian Refugee Recognition Award. In 2012 Abdi was proud to share the plight of many refugees with similar journeys and the untold story of civil war in Somalia, with his appearance in the award-winning documentary *Go Back To Where You Came From* (Series 2).

Abdi strongly believes that every person has the right to a productive, happy life and that begins with the young people. 'Anything is possible if you try, and try again. I am living proof of that.'

— ABDI

INTRODUCTION

This is the second book about my life. I decided to write it because when I speak at schools, people always ask me about my childhood. I do like to talk about myself, but after I tell the stories over and over and over again, it can get a bit boring, even for me!

In my younger days in Mogadishu, and afterwards leaving Somalia, a lot of things happened to me that I have never forgotten. Some of the things are important and some of the things are not important. Each of them made an impression on me. Some of them are painful, some of them are funny, and some of them are uncomfortable. But all of these things have made me the person I am now.

What do you know about Somalia? Lots of people think it is just full of pirates and camel herders. This is not true. Some people think there are no buildings there. This is also not true. Or maybe the only thing you've heard about Somalia is the war and refugees.

Somalia is so much more.

I know a lot about Western culture, and about Australia, but I feel that people don't know much about Somalia.

So this is also the reason I decided to write this book.

Let me tell you about the Somalia I have known. Back then, before the war. Before everything changed and I found myself at fifteen leaving my home, leaving without my family, and walking across the country to try to stay alive.

DiD YOU KNOW?

Somalia is a small country located on the Horn of Africa. The Horn of Africa is made up of four countries — Djibouti, Ethiopia, Eritrea and Somalia. To the west of Somalia are Ethiopia, Djibouti and Kenya; the Gulf Of Aden is to the north; and the Indian Ocean is to the east. Mogadishu is the capital city.

FROM THE BEGINNING – FAMILY LIFE

I am four years old, and my favourite place is sitting on my grandma's knee. She is feeding me the best bits of the food she is eating. She feeds me first before herself, and before anyone else.

She cooks all the best things for me. Friday in Somalia is like Sunday in Australia. Thursday and Friday are our weekend. On Fridays she cooks me egg and goat's liver fried with onion and capsicum, eaten with banana and a sourdough risen-flatbread called injera.

This grandma is my father's mum, and she lives in the country in a place called Awdiinle. I love this place on her knee, and I love her smell. She and her house smell of sand, the wood fire she cooks on, the trees and the red earth.

She cries with happiness when she sees me. "Nuu-row," she says, hugging me. It's my nickname, and she gave it to me. It means "The Shining One". When she says it, I glow on the inside. She cries at everything I do and say. She hugs me. So many hugs. I take as many as I can get.

She tells me so many stories. She tells me stories about when my dad was young. I sit closer. "More! Tell more stories," I say. I like all the stories: the real ones, the made-up ones, the serious ones and the ones that make me laugh out loud.

My life begins in Mogadishu, which is a big city. It is the capital of Somalia and has been around for hundreds of years. It has long been a tourist destination, with many flocking to see our golden beaches.

Mum is only eighteen when she gives birth to me. She is quite young, but not that young really. Most of my friends' mums are the same age. They sometimes have two children by then.

She almost had to get married when she was sixteen. Her mum and dad said she had to marry a much older man. She didn't want to, so she ran away from home, all the way to Mogadishu. That is where she met my dad.

My mum, Aalima, is happy I am a boy. I am born at a time when everyone in Somalia thinks you are wealthy and successful if you have a son. Everyone wants to have boy babies.

Next she has Jamila, a girl, my sister. Mum loves her, even though she is a girl.

When I am born, my grandma comes from the countryside where she lives. She comes to take care of me. I am her eldest son's first child. This is what grandparents do in Somalia when babies are born. They come to help. The grandfather usually comes as well, and he teaches you things. But my grandfather died when my dad was five years old.

The Somali word for grandma is *ayeeyo* or *abooy*. The Somali word for grandpa is *awoowe* and *aboow*.

As soon as I can walk, I run. I run everywhere. My grandma is short with short legs. She runs after me. She lets me run. Wherever I run, she runs.

When I am two years old, I am running and I fall over. I cry. She cries.

A man passes by. "Oh poor you," he says. He gives me a shilling (like giving someone one dollar).

When Mum finds out what happened, she rolls her eyes. "Embarrassing," she says. "Our family doesn't need that. I can't *believe* that happened to you." (She is often embarrassed by me.)

When I am four years old, my grandma goes back to her home in her village, Awshine. She is sad to leave me, but she is not sad to leave Mogadishu. "It's too busy here," she says, but she will miss me. I miss her. She is the person who loves me no matter what, so she leaves me with something very important. She leaves me with her big, big love, and so I love myself and believe in myself.

Ayeeyo gets blind as she gets older. We visit her. We

don't go very often. It takes about five hours on the bus to Awshine.

"It's me," I tell her when we arrive. "It's Nuurow Isaak Aden." I use all my names like I'm meant to. It's a sign of respect. I am so happy to see her again.

"Nuurow," she says, happy. It has been a long time since we have seen her. She starts to cry. She always cries.

When my other grandma, my mother's mum, sees me, she doesn't cry. She says: "Why so skinny? You need to eat something."

Another time, when I am four years old, we go to visit my mum's mum, my other Ayeeyo. The one who thinks I am too skinny. We catch a bus there. My grandfather's brother (we call him grandfather as well) writes a little note for me because I am sick that day. He makes a special Somali blessing by rolling up the note and putting it in a little piece of leather. He sews it up and gives it to me to wear around my neck.

At the end of the visit, we head back to the bus to go back to Mogadishu.

My mum hurries to take the leather blessing

necklace from around my neck before we get on the bus. "Embarrassing," she says. "So old-fashioned. We do not want to look like we are from the country. We are city people."

We get on the bus and sit down.

I say loudly, 'WHERE'S MY HERSE?" Meaning my note from my grandfather.

Everyone on the bus looks at me. I like that. I give them back a huge smile.

My mum glares at me. "That's it! We have to change buses!" she says. "So embarrassing."

SCHOOL

I am five when I start school early. I can already read and count. A teacher at the school looks at my gums and teeth to check my age, because different teeth come through at different ages. He cannot believe I can already read and count at five years old. Everyone else is six-and-a-half years old when they start school. It is just because I try hard and I really love learning.

It is not compulsory to go to school, but I want to go, and my mum and dad want me to go. They want Jamila and I to be successful and have a good life in Somalia when we get older, maybe having a job in the government. I don't know about that because my dream is to be a professional soccer player, or even a teacher, and I am also keen on owning lots of donkeys. Anyway, I love learning so I love to go to school. I even really love homework.

My primary school is called Siad Barre Government

Primary School. It is named after the president of Somalia. I love my school. I feel lucky to have such a good education. When Mum and Dad were young, there wasn't even a proper school for them to go to. There was only an Italian school. So I feel very lucky.

DiD YOU KNOW?

Major General Mohamed Siad Barre was the leader of the army and part of a group of people who wanted to overthrow the previous government. Siad Barre became president of Somalia in 1969 and remained in that position until 1991.

He was a very popular president for many years.

Education in the Somali language began after Siad Barre made it the official language of Somalia in 1972. The Somali alphabet also became the official alphabet for writing at that time.

I go to school five-and-a-half days of the week. On Thursday we go to school for half-a-day, and on Friday we don't go to school. Friday is like Sunday in Somalia. We go to school for nine months, and then have three months holiday.

I have to be at school at 7 am. I wear a uniform of a white shirt and khaki shorts. It's already hot at this time of the day. I walk to school past shops and stalls selling food. My classroom is in a white Mediterranean-style building. The school is made up of several of these buildings.

There are 51 other students in the classroom with me. I sit at a desk that has a concrete top and wooden legs.

We learn maths, Arabic, Somali language, science, sport, arts and crafts, social studies and geography.

Today we are learning about geography. I love the atlas and I love geography. I love Australia, and I have read all about it.

My teacher, Macallin Yousef (Macallin means "teacher"), says, "Which country has more animals than people?"

I put up my hand. "Australia is such a country," I say.

The other kids and the teacher have hardly heard anything about Australia, but I know many facts. "It is a mostly empty country. It has people, but there are many, many more animals than people."

I am proud that I know something the others do not. This part of my life is a huge coincidence, which I will not realise for many years: that one day I will be familiar with the Australian landscape and the native animals, because I will be living there. I also discuss this in my first book, *Shining: The Story of a Lucky Man*, which you can read when you get older!

We finish school at 1 pm. There are 1500 kids at the school, and we are happy it is over for the day.

It is so hot. Every day it's hot – always close to 40 degrees. I run home through the streets of Mogadishu, past the white Mediterranean-style buildings. I have qaado (lunch) when I get home. Qaado is a big meal, our main meal of the day. Today it is rice and sauce with banana, and I have a big drink of lemon and water (our version of lemonade). We eat lunch on a cloth spread on the floor, and it is quite common for us to use our hands. This is the way people eat in Somalia.

After lunch we have a siesta – a big nap. It is far too hot to do anything else, although sometimes I just read a book or draw instead of sleeping. I read Somali folk stories and draw people and animals.

My mum and dad are not your usual Somali parents. Mum is a businesswoman. She trained as a nurse, but now she buys and sells things. Most other kids' mums don't work. She is the only mum I know who works. My dad, Isak, worked in the hospital too. He trained there from a young age and became the head nurse. Now he is a chef. This means when he is at home he does the cooking. This is not what other kids' dads do. It is the 1980s though, and in Somalia it's normal for dads to go away to work. My dad works for a Somali general, who takes my dad with him to Paris. Dad goes for many years, and doesn't come back very often. This means it is mostly just my mum, my sister and I. Mum works a lot, too, so often it is just my sister Jamila and I. Our aunty looks after us. In Somalia it is very common for relatives or friends to raise you. They often discipline you, too, so you need to be careful, otherwise the lady who sells milk down the road can be telling you off.

It's after school, and my sister and I make lemonade. We do this every day. I squeeze the lemons and she gets the ice. I go to the shop, too. Families don't have electric fridges so we must buy our food every day.

I go to the butcher with gold teeth. I buy goat meat from him. "Hey, Ten On," I say. It's his nickname because he's "on" all the time. You can't turn him off. He gets ten out of ten for talking. He is very lively and talks A LOT.

He remembers me. "MY GOLD TEETH ARE BETTER THAN YOUR TEETH," he booms at me.

I buy an onion, two pieces of garlic, one lemon and tomato paste.

The other kids don't shop for their families, but for me it is normal.

My sister is younger than me, but she is feisty. She is loud. I protect her, but sometimes she doesn't need protecting. We are outside playing. Another kid starts pushing her around and giving her a hard time. "Stop that," I tell him. He punches me hard. Jamilla is mad. She goes over to the kid and bites him through his t-shirt. "That will teach you to punch my brother."

The bite wound gets infected. He has to go to hospital. I think: My sister is awesome.

My dad is here on holiday from his work in Paris, and we are sitting at the table at dinner time. I am about eight years old. I am excited to see him, but also a little

nervous and shy because I do not see him very often. I have got so many questions to ask him. I want him to help me make decisions. Instead I accidentally do a pop-off. (A pop-off is what we call a fart.) Dad laughs. Mum is angry, and she chases me with a stick from the tree. Luckily I am faster than my mum. (Though she gets lots of practice because she chases me a lot.) I look back at my dad. He smiles at me, and I smile back. I am happy.

We live in a cream house made of bricks with a courtyard in the centre. A big gate opens out onto the courtyard, and there is a big tree in the middle that we call an Indian tree. We often spend time under this tree, especially in the afternoons when it is the hottest.

We first moved here from another part of Mogadishu when I was about six years old. We used to live in a house made of wood and mud and cow poo; it was a bit like a mud-brick house. Then my parents had this one built. The old house didn't have electricity or a phone, but our new house has these things.

The new house has five bedrooms, where we sleep on metal beds with mattresses. There is also a room where we eat, and a shower and toilet. We just have cold showers because it is always so hot in Somalia. There is also an outside toilet and shower. We cook outside, where there is an oven powered by a wood fire and a fridge in the ground. This is a large clay jug that is placed under the ground to keep it cool. My family is not poor. They are not rich. They are somewhere in the middle.

I feel lucky living in Mogadishu. I feel like we have everything we need. It is a good life. I love my school. I love playing soccer. I love my home, my friends.

And I get to watch Chuck Norris movies.

The local cinema in Mogadishu is an open-air cinema, and it plays Chuck Norris movies and Indian Bollywood movies. I like the cinema and I really like Chuck Norris.

I am ten years old. Mum doesn't like me going to the movies but she sometimes works until 8 pm. She won't know if I go. So after dinner (and of course I do my homework first), I sneak away from home to go to the movies. But I don't have any money, so I have to be an action hero like Chuck Norris and climb a big tree so I can see the movie. I take a pillow with me to make the tree a bit more comfortable, and watch the movie from the tree. The movies are American but they are made with a different soundtrack so it looks like Chuck Norris is speaking Italian. Then there are Somali subtitles that people can read to understand what is going on.

DiD YOU KNOW?

Italy took over Mogadishu in 1905 and made Mogadishu the capital of what they called "Italian Somaliland". The Italians called the city Mogadiscio.

In the 1960s the Italians handed over our country to the Somalis, and Somalia became independent.

The whole time, I think Chuck Norris is not an American but is actually Italian! I only find out he is not Italian when the cinema starts playing the movies with the soundtrack dubbed in Somali instead of Italian. Chuck Norris is always the hero in the movies and he always wins. I think that I would like to be a hero who wins.

One day I find film negatives from a movie just lying in the street. All the other kids gather around as I get a light and shine it through the negatives so we can see the pictures. The other kids are amazed.

Sometimes I make soccer balls, too. I find busted, abandoned soccer balls and use the pieces to make a new one. The kids line up to get my soccer balls. They trade things like chocolate milk powder to get them. All the kids love soccer and there aren't enough good soccer balls around, so my soccer balls are in demand.

It is the afternoon. School has finished and the sun is going down. I go next door to knock on my second-best-friend Ali's door so he knows it's time for soccer. We play soccer every evening with the other neighbourhood kids. The only time we don't play soccer is when we go to watch soccer. Big teams from other countries come to play the Somali team. I want to

be a soccer player when I get older. The other boys do, too.

My team is called Nuurow, of course, after my nickname Nuurow. There are ten players. Nine are boys and there is one girl. This is not common. She asks to play and I say yes, because why not? She is a good player, even better than the boys.

I introduce her to the team. Her name is Farhiya.

If anyone complains about there being a girl playing for us, they are out of the team. Out!

I am playing outside with my neighbour, Hawo, and we are kicking her soccer ball around when a big kid comes. He is much older than us, about 22, and he is a big guy. He just takes her ball. I am skinny and small, but I can't bear it. I say, "Give her back the ball."

He doesn't give back the ball. Instead, he gives me a big punch, a very big punch that makes me dizzy, and then I fall to the ground. It knocks me out. My jaw hurts like anything. It is sore and swollen for weeks.

One Friday, I am excited because this is the day of the big game. We go to the main stadium in Mogadishu to see top African soccer teams come to play the Somali team. Even international teams come – the Italians, the English and other African teams such as Kenya. I go to the stadium to watch soccer with my friends whenever I can.

LIFE IN MOGADISHU

I am twelve. It's Friday afternoon and, like every Friday, two friends and I head for the Indian Ocean. The beach is less than a kilometre from my house in Mogadishu. Like most days in Somalia, it's sizzling hot, at least 35 degrees. On our way, we climb the big sand dunes and run down the other side towards the cool, inviting water.

We stop just short of the water.

"Hey Ali, can you smell that?" I can smell a terrible smell. My dad always tells me, "If you smell a terrible smell at the beach, just run."

Dad was spot on. What we could smell was crocodile.

"DON'T GET IN! RUN!' I yell out to the other boys.

"Oh, you're just being a coward. Come in," the boys call back, and they dive into the waves.

Then they see the crocodile and start to splash

about. They are frantic. They rush to get back to shore. I wade in to help them. Once back on dry land, we finally take my dad's advice and run.

(That's not the only traumatic thing that happened to me at that beach. Once I saw my maths teacher swimming with no clothes on.)

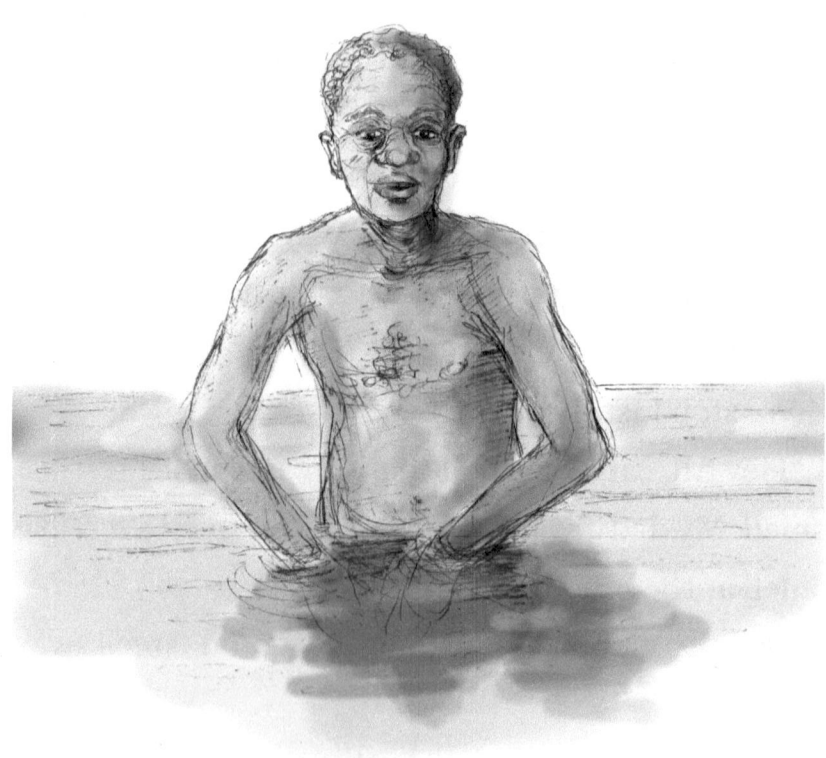

I might not like the crocodiles roaming free in the ocean, but I love the animals at the agricultural show at the showground in Mogadishu. My uncles take me there, and once my dad took me there. We feed the cows and goats, and look at the displays of tractors and other farm machinery.

I want to go back to a tent where there is an educational video playing on a television screen. The video shows a European woman having a baby. "Come on," I say to my friends, "we can learn something." I am eleven and curious, and I want to learn, but I also can't believe it – we can see someone's bottom right there on the TV! But my friends don't want to go.

DiD YOU KNOW?

Mogadishu used to be known as the White Pearl of the Indian Ocean. It was established in the first century. Australia was first settled in the 18th Century.

Somalia has beautiful beaches. In the 1960s, before a military coup and the war, Mogadishu was a popular tourist destination.

Every time I see a small shop or I see someone riding a donkey, I say to Mum "I'm going to have my own shop one day. I'm going to have a lot of donkeys and run a business."

"How embarrassing," Mum says. "Be quiet. We're not like the lower classes. They are the ones who have donkeys."

But I don't mind. I just think about having my own business.

Sometimes I hitch a ride from a donkey and cart carrying vegetables or building materials through Mogadishu. I hold on underneath the cart so the owner doesn't see me. Whenever he catches me, he hits me with a stick, but it's worth it because it means I get shade from the hot sun, too. Double bonus.

I also like to hitch a ride from the fire truck. It's more dangerous than the donkey cart, but it's faster and I need a ride. I hop on the back of the truck as it drives past. We bump across the streets; the main streets are of bitumen, and other streets are crushed rock and sand. The fire truck takes me a few kilometres and then I get off. Thanks for the free ride.

Like everyone in Somalia, I love stories and poetry.

My good friend, Ali, lives next door. His dad tells the best stories. I don't care if they are true or not. I just love them. When the stories make me laugh, I love them even more.

It is that time again. Like every week, we gather around Ali's dad. We are excited and wait eagerly for his latest story. I start by sitting on the outside of the small group of people. As he tells the story, I move closer and closer, inching across the floor, until

I am right underneath him. I am so caught up in the story that I don't realise I'm moving. I arrive at his feet and stare up at him open-mouthed, drinking in every word.

Of course, I am not quiet during the story. I have so many questions and they can't wait. I am bursting with questions. I just yell them out when I think of them.

"There was a married couple," Ali's dad begins. "The wife hears that her husband is not going to work, but he is sneaking off with his friends to drink coffee and watch soccer. The wife is mad. She thinks, I must find out if this is true. How can I find out?

So she finds a young girl, only twelve. She tells her, 'You need to pretend you are deaf so that my husband does not know that you can talk.' This is part of the wife's plan. The wife is a weather girl. She has to look for the weather before it hits town so she can tell everyone. She tells the girl, 'I have to go to do my weather job. I'll be away for three days. When you find out what is happening, meet me halfway so you can tell me.' So the girl finds out the truth and meets the wife halfway to tell her the news. 'It's true,' she tells the wife."

"WHAT ABOUT THE WIFE?" I interrupt loudly.

"Quiet!" all the other people in the room yell at me.

"BUT did SHE drink coffee and chat with her friends when she went to the weather job?"

I'm not going to be quiet when I have burning questions inside me.

"Abdi, shhhhhh." It's my mum, telling me to be quiet, but she thinks it is funny. She is laughing.

Ali's dad does a big sigh. "Abdi, that is not the point."

"But..."

"Abdi, shhhhhh."

DiD YOU KNOW?

Somalia has a long history of storytelling and poetry. Somali people are great storytellers and poets. A lot of Somali history, culture and beliefs are told as stories and these are passed down from old people to young people. It is part of what keeps Somali culture alive.

Since the Somali language did not exist in a written form until 1972, the Somali people acquired the skill of memorising and speaking, and can tell stories for many hours.

When I am finally quiet, he continues with the story.

"So back at home the wife hides under the hay and she has the Quran with her. She opens it and starts reading it like poetry. It is the middle of the day and the husband is meant to be at work. The young girl has told her he is coming home. He thinks she is at her weather job. When he arrives and is close to the haystack, the wife jumps out of the hay and chases him, yelling at him to come back and face the music."

I laugh and laugh at this. I love a good chasing! (But I still have questions.)

On my way home from school I stop at Aunty Khadijo's house. I go there often to help her. She is very old and has lived there for a long time.

When I go to her house, she gives me tea to drink, but sometimes there is an ant in the tea so I only pretend to drink it. I'm not going to eat the ant. Plus it's very hot weather all day every day in Somalia. Even in hot weather, Somali people still love hot tea, and I never understand this.

"Abdi, you must count my money," the old lady says to me. She goes to get her money from a secret hiding place, and hands all her Somali shillings over to me. "You are the only one I trust," she says.

She doesn't trust her family, but she trusts me to count her money. She can definitely trust me. Plus I am good at counting. I am fast, but I know a boy who has six fingers on each hand and six toes on each foot. People tease him, but I don't tease him. I respect him. He can count money much faster than me.

DID YOU KNOW?

Somali money used to be the Somalo when Somalia was controlled by Italy. Their cultural influences can be still seen today, with many Somali dishes including pasta and tomatoes. Some words that Somali people use also have Italian origins, such as ice-cream, which we call gelato.

LANGUAGE

One of the other kids has written some graffiti on our house. They have written "Abdi Ciyaal Suuq". It means "Abdi is a market child." This is a mean thing to call someone. A "market child" is a dirty, homeless child with no parents who always has flies on his face and hangs around the market. My mum sees the graffiti. I think maybe she is mad because she doesn't like that someone has called her son a market child. But, no.

"Abdi! Look! Someone has put graffiti on my wall. The wall is ruined. So bad. Embarrassing."

But Mum is never worried about me. She knows I am smart and can run very fast. I am a skinny kid but I can stand up for myself, and I do.

In Somalia we always give people nicknames. These nicknames are not very polite and they stick for life, but in Somalia it's normal. If you have a big head, you might be called "Sarah Goon", which means "Sarah with the huge head". The nickname is not always a description of a body part. I know someone called "Coryaan", which means disabled or one-leg; another guy is called Diarrhea, because once he pooed his pants; a few people are called Alooley, which means the big belly guy; and I have heard about someone called "Field Goal", like a soccer goal, because he has a large gap between his front teeth. The nicknames in Somalia can be quite harsh; however sometimes it is just descriptive and an easy way to tell the boys called the same name apart. A name like big belly in Somalia is one you are proud of, because it means you have wealth. My nickname is sometimes "Skinny", but I think it should be changed to "Handsome": Abdi the handsome one.

"Abdi," my mum calls out. "Have you cleaned your teeth?"

Usually in Somalia, if we want to swear we have done something, or swear we are telling the truth, we say, "Walahi bilahi". It means "I swear to God." Instead, I say to Mum, "Malay bilahi." It sounds pretty much the same when it comes out of your mouth, but it means "I swear to fish."

She thinks I'm saying, "I swear to God".

This way I figure I am not troubling God, and I'm not troubling my mum.

I boast to my friends, "My dad can speak another language."

"No, that's rubbish," they say.

But Dad visits from Paris and I say to him, "Say something to my friends in Italian."

Yes, Italian, not French.

DiD YOU KNOW?

The official languages of Somalia are Somali and Arabic.

Somali lost its ancient way of writing words over hundreds of years. A number of different ways of writing Somali have been used over the years, but President Siad Barre made the Somali alphabet the main way of writing the language in 1972.

The Somali language uses all letters of the English alphabet except p, v and z.

I am talking with my friend about playing soccer, but I don't only use Somali to communicate. I also use my hands and my head. "We'll play over there," I say, and point with my chin instead of my finger.

He touches his thumb to his fingers and shakes it side to side. He is asking me: "Where?"

I point with my chin again.

He flicks his own chin with his thumb. He is saying it is too busy to play soccer there.

We talk fast and loudly and wave our hands around. Maybe that's because Italy is a big part of Somalia's history, and the Italians use their hands so much when they talk.

"You can be the goalkeeper today," I say. I push the side of my nose with my finger. It means he has to do it.

He opens his hand and sticks the first finger against his temple. He's saying I'm crazy. "We'll never win if I'm the goalie," he says.

I talk with my hands, as most of us do. I don't like it when Mum talks with her hands though; they move very fast and look like a helicopter. I get worried she might get too close to someone, and she will accidentally hit them.

DID YOU KNOW?

Many older Somali people speak Italian because the Italians made Somalia an Italian colony from 1905 to the 1960s.

Many Somalis speak Arabic because Somalia has been connected to the Arab World countries for many years through trading. Also because everybody in Somalia watches and reads the Arabic media, and has to go to Dugsi, or religious school.

RELIGION AND CULTURE

Religion is a big part of my life in Mogadishu. It is a big part of everyone's lives. It doesn't matter if we believe or not; it is just part of how we live.

We have to go to Dugsi every day. Dugsi is Islam school, where we have to memorise the Quran, and write it on bits of wood. The Dugsi Macallin (the teacher) is mean and hits us with a stick when we get things wrong.

I don't like Dugsi. We have to sit on the dirty sand. It sticks to my legs and gets stuck between my toes. Today I do not want to go to Dugsi. I play in the street instead. This is much more fun. I am having a really good time, and I'm so happy not to be at Dugsi getting sand between my toes.

Only then, oh no, my mum is coming towards me, walking along the street. She hasn't noticed me yet. I'm scared she will see me. She will know I am not at Dugsi. She can't find out. She will chase me with the stick, and worse, she will tell the Dugsi teacher and I will have to go to Dugsi detention.

I panic. I need to hide. There isn't anywhere to hide. What should I do? Quick! What should I do?

The only thing I can think of to do is just hold my breath and stick my head in the sand. So that is what I do.

I hold my breath. I can hear her footsteps on the sand as she passes by.

I'm lucky. It worked. She didn't think it was me and walked on by.

Although now I have sand stuck in my nose and mouth, instead of between my toes.

Another day, I am walking down a street in Mogadishu. I see some kids beating a dog with sticks.

"Stop that!" I yell, and run over to rescue the dog.

I pull it away from the kids. "Come on," I urge the dog. It runs with me, and the kids chase me, but I'm good at running. I've had lots of practice.

I get home and tie the dog to the tree in the courtyard at our house. My uncle sees I have a dog, and he is very angry. He has never been so angry with me before; he looks like he is dragon breathing fire. Today he shouts at me, "You should know not to touch dogs! Don't you know this?" I cry. Mum is not home. She is working.

She comes home and finds me crying. I tell her the story. She explains that in the Somali culture, dogs are thought to be unclean. This is because many are wild. In Somali culture, if you touch a dog you have to wash seven times.

My uncle and my mum make me return the dog to the people who were beating it. This makes me very sad.

DiD YOU KNOW?

Most people in the country are Muslim, with most people being a kind of Muslim called Sunni. The Muslim religion is Islam, and Sunni Islam is the largest group of Islam.

Sunni Islam is the religion that has the most followers in the world.

CLANS AND TRIBES

I am part of the tribe called Rahanweyn. This tribe is not from Mogadishu. I don't tell anyone what my tribe is. I try to hide it because when I walk through the streets of Mogadishu, I hear, "All you Rahanweyn are so stupid." The kids say it. They hear their parents say it. Their parents hear their parents say it.

I am not stupid, but Somali people have been saying, "All Rahanweyn are stupid" for such a long time that they don't even think about why they say it anymore.

My clan is Helede, like my father. My mother's clan is Xariin.

The war is coming. We all know it is coming. People fear the other tribes. We start to feel the tension in the air. We hear people talking. We notice things happening around Mogadishu. We hear bombs going off. We see people with guns.

The government soldiers are taking young boys to fight the other tribes (see note below) – I know this because my cousins have already been taken. I pretend I have a limp when I see the soldiers, because they won't take the ones who are disabled.

I am scared. I do not want to get separated from my family. I used to look everyone in the eyes and give them a big smile, but now I just look down.

We record ourselves talking to Dad and send the tapes to him in Paris. "Somalia is getting worse, Dad," I say on the tape. "It's very scary."

DiD YOU KNOW?

A Somali person has a tribe and a clan. A Somali's tribe is the place they are from.

Their clan is like their last name – the clans formed from family groups a long time ago in Somalia. In Somalia you can tell a person's clan from their last name, and also from the way they speak or act.

DID YOU KNOW?

When there was peace in Somalia the people were more relaxed about their tribal differences, but then the government started fighting different tribes. The government was made up primarily of the one tribe and they wanted to rule all of Somalia. The government was favouring different tribes, and fighting against others.

My dad finally comes back to Mogadishu with his employer, the army general. He works for the general at his house.

The government soldiers have divided Mogadishu in half with a barrier made of concrete blocks and razor wire. Dad is on one side; I am on the other. I can't see or speak to him. I feel so scared.

Mum is working in Italy. I ring her. "Please come back, Hooyo. I'm scared we will be killed. There are bombs going off everywhere."

"You are safe," she says, but she is wrong.

DID YOU KNOW?

At the end of the 1980s, the Somali army was fighting the tribes in the north, but by the time the 1990s came along, the Siad Barre regime was losing power.

The tribes' armies eventually overthrew the Barre government in 1991, but that wasn't the end of it. All of the tribes were competing against each other for power, and there wasn't one person like Siad leading the country.

THE WAR

One afternoon my life changes in a big way in just fifteen minutes. As usual, I go to knock on Ali's door. It's a big wooden door, like most of the doors in Somalia. Ali is my second-best friend because I have another one. Just joking, they are all my good friends!

"Ali," I call loudly.

"Hi, Nuurow," Ali says. "I have to do a job for my mum. I'll come later."

"Okay, see you there."

I go to play soccer without him. Fifteen minutes later there is a big explosion. There is dust everywhere. I can't see my house. I can't see Ali's house. I can't tell whether the explosion has hit my family's house or Ali's house.

The war has started. I am thirteen years old. As the dust clears, I see Ali's house is now a pile of rubble. In this moment, I lose my good friend, my ambition to be a soccer player, the rest of my childhood, and my home.

If Ali had come to play soccer with me, he would not have died. His mum died, too.

My dad is still stuck on the other side of the barrier. My mum is still in Italy working, and has not promised anytime she will be coming home. My sister is staying with a friend of our family.

So Mum and Dad don't know where I am. I don't know if my sister is alive.

No one knows what will happen next.

I panic. I run around looking for my sister. People are screaming loudly and crying. I will never forget the sound of those screams.

I find my neighbour. She is the one that people go to for advice. Her name is Aunty Khatijo.

"We are leaving, Abdi," she says. "It is too dangerous here. Where are your mum and dad?"

When I tell her, she pleads with me: "You must come with us. I can't leave you here alone."

I know she is right. I can't stay in Mogadishu on my own. It is too dangerous.

So I leave with her and her children. I have nothing. I leave with nothing, only the clothes on my back.

Lots of other people come, too. We start walking towards Kenya. Kenya is next to Somalia, but it is a long way from Mogadishu. It is almost 500 kilometres away. This is our only option from the southern part of Somalia. However, there is no thought-out plan, we just need to flee. We don't know when we begin that it will take approximately three months to walk there.

There are more than 300 of us walking. Many are women and children. My neighbour has five children. I help her with the children as we walk. We realise it is very dangerous to move about in this way. Soldiers might shoot us if they are suspicious of what we are doing.

Everywhere there are men with guns. We can't trust them. We are all scared we will be killed, too. I wish my mum and dad were here. I just want to be back at home, safe, with Mum and Dad and Jamila and our normal life. But that life has gone.

We are trying to escape the city and the crazy soldiers. It seems like everyone else is, too. The soldiers hurt and kill a lot of people. Sometimes for small things. Sometimes the reason they kill them does not make sense. The soldiers steal things, too. I am just a kid. I am terrified.

The only important thing now is to try to stay alive.

One reason I can survive is because I know all the tribes. I can tell a person's tribe when I meet them. So when I meet the crazy soldiers, I pretend I am the same tribe as them. This saves me from being harmed. I cannot stop some of my friends being harmed.

Sometimes trucks stop to pick us up, but mostly we walk. It is hard to find food and places to sleep. We beg people for food and money. There are so many of us. We are already refugees, but we do not think of ourselves as refugees.

Aunty says to me "Nuurow, when will the sun come back?" She doesn't mean the real sun. That still stays the same. It makes the days hot. She means, "When will we be able to live our lives again and be happy?" All of the groups and individual people are trying to get a ride on the one truck that passes from time to time, and people are trying to navigate a path to safety. Some people know places they can stay to get rest while others don't. During this time, Aunty Khatijo and I start to travel separately.

When we finally arrive at the border with Kenya, after many weeks, there are only five people left from more than 300 people. Some people have died. Other people said they couldn't keep walking

One of the women I have been walking with says, "Come with me, Abdi, I can't find my family." She had five children and, when we get to the border, only one child is left. The other four died because they did not have enough to eat. It is so horrible. I think: I have nothing to worry about. She lost her four children.

We have arrived in Kenya. Yet it is not the end. In some ways it is just the beginning.

DID YOU KNOW?

The conflict in Somalia meant many people had to leave where they lived and be without a home. There are about 1.5 million Somalis still in Somalia without a home, and more than 650,000 living as refugees in camps today in other countries nearby.

Since civil war broke out in the early 90s, approximately 500,000 people have died in Somalia.

Since 2012, there has been a new government in Somalia. The United Nations helped to set it up. Somalia is slowly becoming more stable, but the new government has had to fight often against terrorist groups that want to take over. This still makes the country unsafe for its people.

THE JOURNEY CONTINUES ...

I left my home country and became a refugee. The scary journey didn't end in Kenya. I travelled to Romania and stayed in a refugee camp in Romania for one year. Then I travelled to Germany, and eventually found a way to come to Australia by travelling on another man's passport, pretending to be his son. I was almost sixteen when I arrived.

I eventually found and was reunited with my mum six years later, because the Red Cross organisation helped me. And then I found my sister, but my dad died in the war in Somalia.

Only two people from my Mogadishu school class survived. I was one of them.

I have finished university and worked as a youth worker. I have started my own business as a public speaker, talking at many schools and workplaces. I am now an ambassador for the Red Cross, and I travel Australia talking about my experiences.

ABDI'S ADVICE FOR LIFE

I have written this book because I am often asked by younger people what my experiences in Somalia were like. One of my greatest ongoing achievements is my ability to help young people who may not have experienced civil war but are at a crossroads, dealing with difficult issues and feeling like giving up.

Every young person has a journey that will have many ups, downs, speed humps, ladders and elevators. This is what I have learnt from my experiences. This is my advice for you about life.

* **Number 1.** It's really important to make positive choices. Live your life so you are happy.

* People give up. I didn't. Don't give up.

* When you have a problem, you can become strong and bounce back, or you can go the other way. You can shut down and give up.

Instead, try to become strong. There is always a resolution to a problem.

*   You may go through some very tough things and times. Those times will make you stronger, and the person you become will benefit.

*   Independence is one of my favourite words. You can become whatever you want to be.

*   Australia is safe. It is a great place to strive and do well. Australia is a good place to be, but you need to work hard for yourself.

*   Australia will give you a ladder to climb as high as you like. Make sure you do not wait for the elevator.

*   Success for me is not being paid more money so you can buy more stuff. Success is loving what you do and being happy.

* Everyone has fears, and your fears are often your warning alarms that something is wrong. However, do not be afraid to face them. We all have a voice that can be heard.

* Being brave is a huge milestone and personal medal. Protect it well and keep it safe.

* We are all the same; you are as good as anybody.

* Goals are always achievable if you work hard. Sometimes it may feel like you did not reach your goal. However, you did; it was just that your goal changed.

* People ask me, "How come you're so successful?" My answer is: work hard and keep learning.

* You have to like yourself deep down inside: not just the outside, the inside, too.

* Keep learning.

* Respect is important. It works like a two way street; without the cars staying in their lanes they will crash. One of my favourite things is to treat others with respect, and I find that this is often returned with respect.

* Never judge yourself by your failures. They are your speed humps on your journey to success. They are warning signs that are telling you to slow down and learn what you may have done wrong.

* Never hide who you are; be proud of your tribe, clan, or where you have come from. I am proud to be from Somalia and to have been a refugee. To be a refugee is not a bad/dirty word. This is just a word which describes your circumstances at that time, and it has made me the person I am today.

* Do not be afraid to admit your mistakes. It is easier to learn from them.

* Like in the movies, sometimes you're the hero, and sometimes you're the guy who helps the hero. You can't always be the main guy, and often they are more handsome anyway.